Origins

PRE-PREP

Blast Off to Mars!

Adrian Bradbury

Contents

OXFORD
UNIVERSITY PRESS

Congratulations!

You have been chosen to be one of the first humans to visit the planet Mars.

You will blast off to Mars in twenty years' time. That may seem like a long wait, but you have a lot of training to do.

Professor Sara Tanaka will be your special instructor. In this book you will find out about space travellers of the past. You will also find out more about your own mission.

The countdown has begun.
Good luck!

Maria Hoffman
Director,
World Space Organization

Professor Sara Tanaka

Space missions

Sending humans into space is expensive and dangerous. Back in the 1950s, nobody was sure if humans could survive in space. As a test, they sent animals instead!

1957 Laika the dog was sent into **orbit** on board the Russian spacecraft Sputnik 2. Sadly, she died after just a few hours in space, from overheating and stress.

Laika in her space capsule

1961 Russian astronaut Yuri Gagarin was the first human in space. He survived! His spacecraft orbited the Earth once and the mission lasted less than two hours.

1969 American astronauts were the first humans to land on the Moon.

Astronauts brought back rocks to help gather information.

Where are you going?

Twelve people have stood on the surface of the Moon, but we cannot live on the Moon as it has no water and only a thin **atmosphere**. To find another planet that we can live on, we need to travel further – to Mars.

The surface of Mars is rocky and covered in red dust.

How long will you stay?

The distance between Earth and Mars changes as they travel around the Sun. Spacecraft can only travel from Earth to Mars during the short time when the two planets are close together. By the time your mission gets to Mars, the planets will already be drifting apart. You will need to stay on Mars until they get close together again. That means you will be there for at least one and a half years.

Mars

Earth

🪐 Your mission:

Your mission is to find out what it is like to live on another planet.

We have chosen Mars because:

- it is not too far from Earth
- it is not too hot or as cold as other planets
- we think there could be water in the soil
- there is enough **gravity** to keep you on the ground.

How will you be trained?

Astronauts need to be trained in many skills. It's like being an **engineer**, scientist and doctor all rolled into one. They need to operate a lot of machines on board their spacecraft. They must be able to act quickly when there is a problem and fix it themselves. Most astronauts carry out scientific tests in space, too.

This astronaut is working on a medical experiment in space.

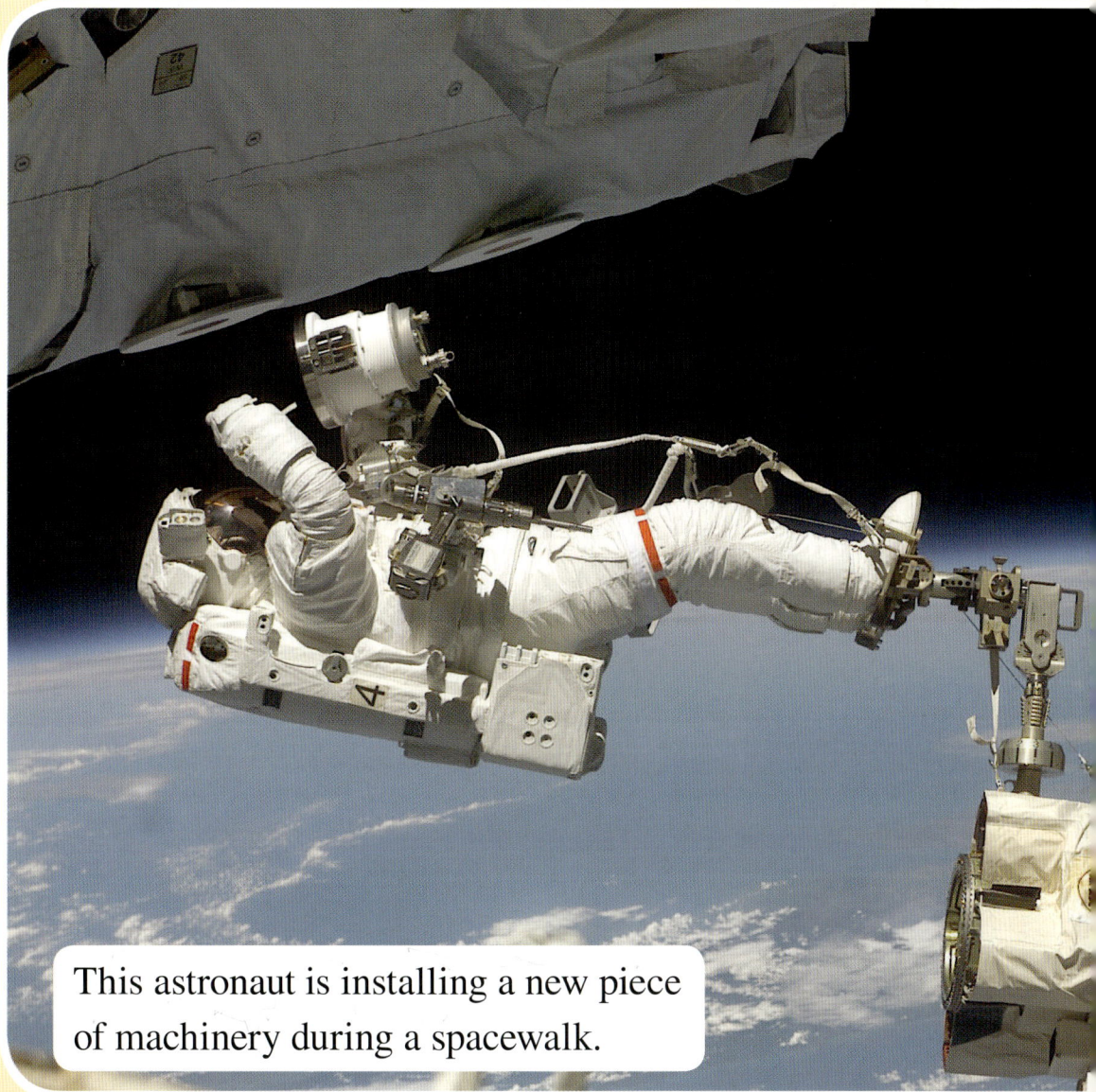

This astronaut is installing a new piece of machinery during a spacewalk.

As the UK astronaut Tim Peake said, "You're up there by yourself. There's no doctor, there's no computer engineer – so you have to learn all of these skills."

Tim Peake trained for six years before going into space. He did a lot of training in a **simulator**. This lets you tackle all the problems you might find in space – without the danger! He also trained underwater, in caves, in freezing conditions and in zero gravity. You need a strong body and a strong mind to survive in space.

training underwater

inside a simulator

training in zero gravity

🪐 Your mission:

You will probably be in a team of four or six people, all trained in different skills in case of emergencies:

- computer operation
- engineering
- electronics
- science
- medical skills.

How will you get there?

Although your spacecraft will be an ultra-modern design, the basics will be quite similar to the very first spacecraft.

The first astronauts who went to the Moon lived in this Apollo module.

There will be a small section for you to live and work in. There will probably be a separate section for food and equipment.

Beneath all this there will be gigantic rockets and fuel tanks to blast you into space. Once you are in space these huge rockets are not needed any more, so they will drop off. Your power will then come from a small engine and solar panels.

Apollo module

This Saturn V rocket sent the first humans to the Moon.

Early spacecraft only needed to take astronauts a fairly short distance, either to the Moon or to the **International Space Station**.

Scientists are now developing spacecraft that can take people much further, to explore deep space. Powerful on-board computers will steer you all the way to Mars.

engines

NASA's Space Launch System

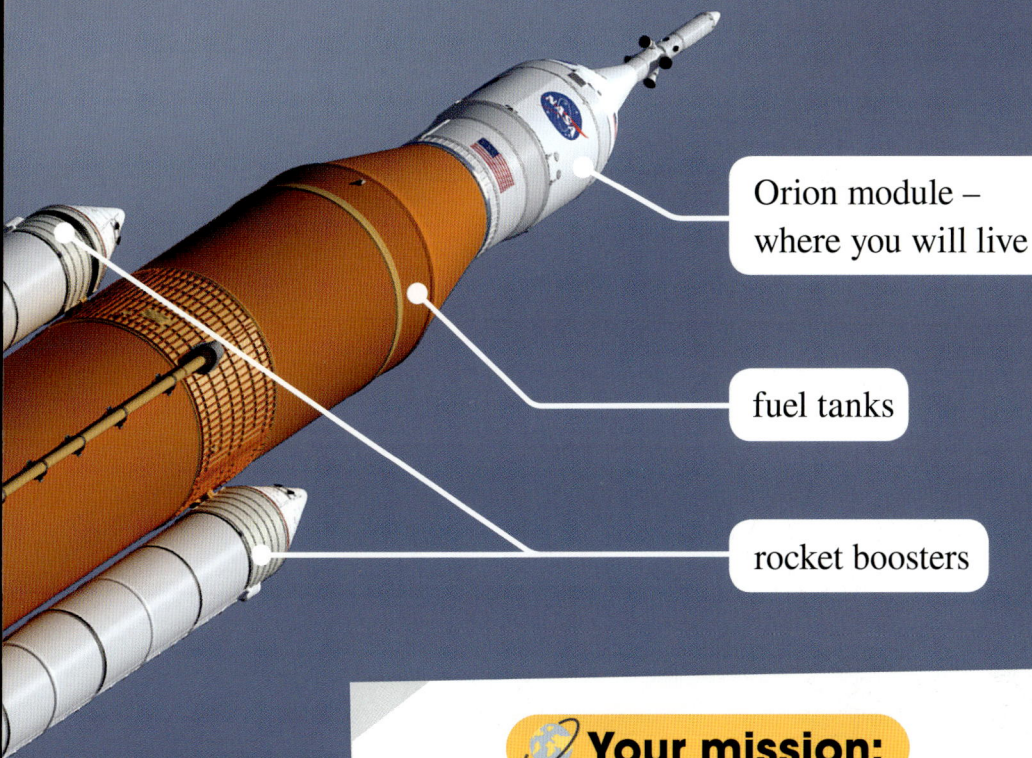

Orion module – where you will live

fuel tanks

rocket boosters

🌀 Your mission:

Your spacecraft could look like the Space Launch System. It had its first test flight in 2014.

However, technology is developing all the time. When your mission begins, spacecraft designs may be completely different!

What will your journey be like?

Travelling through space is not easy. There's very little room on spacecraft and that means astronauts live close together, often for a long time.

Orion module

There isn't enough room to carry all the **oxygen** and water that's needed for the journey. Machines recycle the air and water so that it can be used again and again.

Astronauts use a model of the Orion module to train for possible missions to Mars.

There is almost no gravity on board, so astronauts float around – unless they are strapped in or holding on to something.

Astronauts move around by floating.

To keep their muscles strong, astronauts need to exercise a lot while on board – often for up to three hours each day.

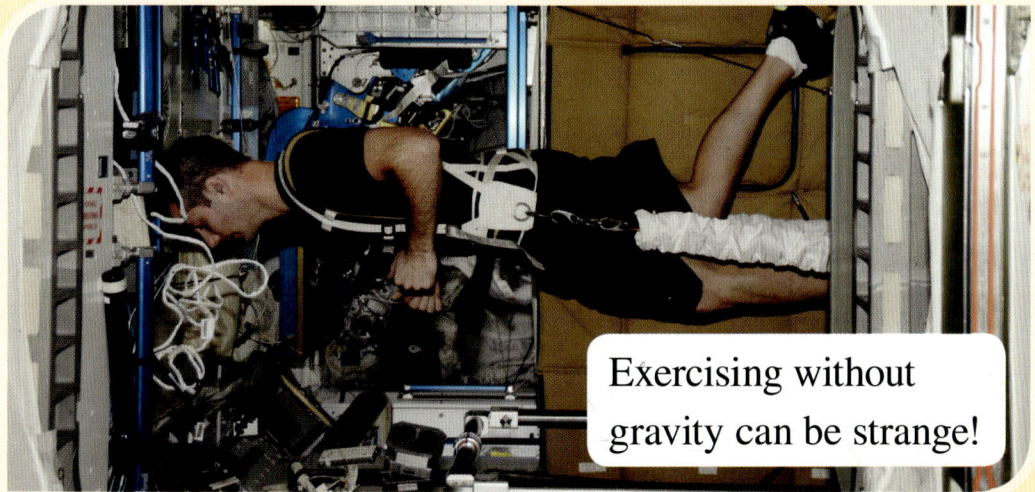

Exercising without gravity can be strange!

🪐 Your mission:

Your journey to Mars will last between six and eight months, which is a long time – so you'd better get along with the other astronauts!

The journey is tough, but landing on Mars is the most dangerous part. It will be difficult to slow your spacecraft down and stop it crashing – but don't worry! We have our top scientists working on that problem.

What will you do on Mars?

There have already been several **unmanned** missions to Mars. Four rover robots have been able to explore and send back photos. They have sent lots of useful information.

Sojourner – launched in 1996

Spirit – launched in 2003

Opportunity – launched in 2003

Curiosity – launched in 2011

More unmanned craft will go to Mars. They will take food supplies and machines to help set up a base. They may also find out new things about Mars that we don't know yet. Robots will be sent to set up some buildings and roads before any astronauts arrive.

Robots could construct buildings using 3D printing.

Keep in touch!

It takes anywhere between 4 minutes and 24 minutes for a radio message to get to Earth from Mars. This depends on how far apart the two planets are at the time.

There is only a tiny amount of oxygen in the atmosphere, but scientists think they can solve this problem. They have developed machines that can produce oxygen from another gas found on Mars. This means that you will be able to breathe. You should be able to grow food too, but that will take time.

🌍 Your mission:

You will start to build a **community** base for all the Mars travellers that will follow you. At first you will probably live and work in your spacecraft, or in a giant **inflatable** dome. Later, you might use the rocks on Mars to make other buildings. You might also drill down into the rock to build shelters underground.

Our instructors will prepare you carefully, but even the cleverest scientists don't really know what will happen when you get to Mars. It will be both exciting and rather scary.

Still up for the challenge?
Then get ready for BLAST OFF!

This could be your home on Mars!

Glossary

atmosphere the gases surrounding the surface of a planet

community people living and working together

engineer someone who designs or fixes machines

gravity the force that pulls things towards the ground

inflatable filled with air

International Space Station spacecraft that orbits around the Earth, with a science laboratory on board

orbit travel in space around the Earth, a star or a planet

oxygen the part of the air that we need to survive

simulator a machine where astronauts can pretend they are in space and practise their skills

unmanned without astronauts on board

Index